Spectral Reflections

Kirstyn Baker

BookLeaf Publishing
India | USA | UK

Presentation by *BookLeaf Publishing*

Web: www.bookleafpub.com

E-mail: info@bookleafpub.com

ISBN : 9789357448062

First edition 2021

DEDICATION

This book is dedicated to all we have lost and the memories that still remain.

ACKNOWLEDGEMENT

Many thanks to my parents, Terry and Sandra, for feeding my obsession with stories all these years. To my furry sidekicks Milo and Zeus, for their trusty supervision. Lastly, a huge thank you to Zoe, my rock, editor and friend, without whom this book would never have been possible.

PREFACE

Many of these poems come from my own personal experiences. Some are inspired by events and experiences of others and some are fictional. In all of the poems in this book, the feelings are very real and have resonated with me.

Death and dark topics have been a fascination for me for a long time and I learnt from a young age the meaning of death and, as I expanded my interests from monsters to ghosts and the supernatural, I found myself writing about the natural and supernatural elements of death.

Within these pages, dear reader, you will find darkness and light, happiness and sorrow, natural and supernatural and the one inevitability of life... death.

The Oldest Job

Among the living, I have walked
For many thousands of years
Some are scared and some welcome the thought
Many have cried and shed a billion tears

My job is grim and lonely
But it is a burden I must bear
Take a day off? If only
The weight of it is always there

First, a child's soul
I carry in my arms
His mother weeps, his sisters bawl
I hold his soul until he calms

Next, a soldier, brave and strong
Fallen protecting his troop
Wherever he goes, he need not wait long
Another bright soul I must scoop

A murderer on death row
He is next on the list
I watch as the poison does flow
His soul black in the swirling mist

My job is the oldest
Of all known to man
Though it is far from the best
No end in sight since it began

Please, please let me rest

Goodnight

I hold your hand tight
A kiss on the forehead
Like I always do at night
I lay down next to you in our bed

I hold your hand tight
And watch as your eyes close
I dim down the light
Watching as you doze

I hold your hand tight
As your breath starts to slow
No more energy for the fight
I know you want to let go

I hold your hand tight
As your heart slows its beat
Your face turning white
From your body goes the heat

I hold your hand tight
As my own eyes droop shut
Losing all my might
In pieces, my heart is cut

I hold your hand tight
As I wish to follow you
Felling my own soul take flight
Wanting eternity for us two

My hand goes slack
As I watch from above
Then a light touch on my back
There is my love

Welcome The Peace

Boom!
Bomber planes drop their burdens
Boom!
Guns shoot speeding slugs across the field
Boom!
Friends and foes dismembered in seconds
Then...

Bu-boom! Bu-boom!
Sweat dripping, hands shaking
Bu-boom!
Darkness and silence envelop me
Bu-boom
Comforting caresses calm me
Bu-

I welcome the darkness
I welcome the peace

Run

Run
Keep running
Don't stop, he's right there
He's sprinting
Run

Heart pounding
His footsteps close in
Hot breath on my ear
Searing pain

Pain
Burning pain
My flesh dissected
The light fades
Pain

Liar

We twirl around the room
Dancing with no direction
He laughs, no idea of his doom
As he lives without reflection
Soon the light will leave his eyes
Soft hands won't feel her again
The one woman I despise
They met just before ten
Her perfume lingers on his collar
Remnants of lipstick mar his cheek
Whilst I remain here in this squalor
He thinks I am too weak
Too weak to defend my pride
We twirl towards the fire
Too late he sees the anger in my eye
I thrust the poker through this liar

What's Next?

Have you ever wondered about life after death?
What happens when souls leave the earth?
Many questions you have, I can see
Beginning to fester since your birth

Well, come now friend
I'll tell you everything!
Oh don't be shocked
You'll know each single thing

The veil, the process
Yes! Yes! It is all true
Reincarnation, hauntings
And take this book too

Now I know it's a lot
But please try to keep up
I don't have all day
Can't you see the line-up?

Now here is your reading
Start with 'You're Dead: Chapter 1'
Oh no, oh dear
Did you not know your death bell had been rung?

Loyal Friend

Mum's home! Mum's home!
I rush to her side
Maybe she has a bone!
But wait, she's cried
Mummy, what's wrong?
She holds me close
She wasn't gone long
To her head my shoulder is host

I stay as still as I dare
My chin resting on her
Her sorrow too much to bear
I want it as we once were
"She's gone. She's gone"
Mum sobs into me
Gone? Where has she gone?
"Milo, I'm so sorry!"

I start to understand
She's not coming back
I nuzzle mum's hand
Her arms go slack
I will stay with her forever
Never leaving her side
"Milo you are so clever"

A smile she tries to hide

Mum is stronger now
Though her pain I still feel
Without our old pal
But time will soon heal

The Drawing

Everyone is crying
The waiting room fills with tears
Mummy, are you hurt?
She crushes me in a tight hug
Dad is crying, but he doesn't cry
Daddy is strong and tough
Come on sweetheart it's time to go
But I need to show Poppy my drawing!
Daddy takes a deep breath
And leads me down the hall
My Poppy lay there, no more smiles
Though he is sleeping I tell him about
My drawing and all we can do when he is out
The silence is strange, no beeping noises
Say goodbye darling and give him a kiss
I say bye-bye and walk away
The drawing hanging above his bed

Fay

Thongs slap against the linoleum
My heart threatens to burst
Like a racecar full of petroleum
I speed down the hall and curse

The tears, the grief, the pain
Spills out from that room
My family call out my name
Closer and closer the door does loom

I push past my uncles and aunts
Stopping dead in my tracks
I don't believe, I won't, I can't
But there she lay, her face all slack

Her chest barely rising with breath
Her wispy white hair in a mess
I know it's the end but I can't face her death
Some have so much time, others much less

On her head, I plant a kiss
As tears cascade down my face
Her sweet, sweet smile I am going to miss
The monitors show her heartbeat race

And then just like that, she is gone
One last breath leaves her lungs
From my chest, my heart is torn
Somehow the staff are rung

I wail and cry and collapse
She's not gone, she's not gone
In just one second my world snaps
And a new feeling, grief, is born

Buster

Hey there beautiful boy
My precious little man
You haven't touched your food or toy
Stand up Buster, see if you can

In a flurry to the vet
Where the news is dealt
I can't accept it, no, not yet
But oh the pain you have felt

I carry you home in my arms
Lay you on your bed
My head on your chest, keeping you from harm
"You are the best boy," I said

Then comes the time for goodbye
It is so hard to let you go
I sit with you and wonder why
An answer I will never know

You are without pain now
Over the rainbow bridge you'll end
And, my Buster, somehow
We will meet again

Goodbye dear old friend

I Am Not Ready

Eyes open, red as roses
A heavy weight in my chest
Keeps me in bed
I can hear birds chirping
Sun piercing the gloom
Like nothing is wrong
I am not ready

My body protests as I start to move
Emptiness sloshes inside me
Going through the motions now
Shower, brush my teeth
Then hair and some makeup
The black dress I chose threatens to suffocate
I am not ready

Driving up, the church imposing
Friends and family wait
Grief-fill air thick as smoke
Hellos and sorries sound like the chirping
Why do they say sorry?
It sounds so fake
I am not ready

Ushered through the door

I watch everyone go
Lingering in the heat, waiting
Fingers curl around cool brass
Stay strong, head up
Weight on my shoulder lighter than my heart
I am not ready

Like snails we advance up the aisle
Tears spill from overflowing dams
Fists squeeze tighter on my heart
Familiar songs over the speakers
Kind words and memories pierce my heart
Tap, tap it's my turn
I am not ready

Tear-soaked notes crumpled in my hand
Deep breath, deep breath
Glance at the mahogany prison
Her picture smiling on the stand
The silence is heavy and the world grows small
I gaze upon familiar sad faces
I am ready

Ready to say goodbye
Ready to let you go
Ready to accept the pain
Ready to live with your memory

I am ready

Packing

Solemn faces cross the threshold
Packing, sorting and folding
Boxes are labelled keep and be sold
Packing up remnants of a life
Tears fall as memories are restored
Clinging to an old cardigan
Taking memos from the corkboard
Boxes packed away
Everyone tired and resting
It was a hard job done
Like goodbye keeps repeating
The pain is on each face
As fresh as a rosebud bloom
Together they are there in that place
Comforting, caring, crying

Fade

Though the years have past
Time has not begun to heal
But added to the those who passed
My heart aches for you

Some nights the pain is too strong
So I curl up alone and sob
Holding your bear all night long
Your blanket a protective hug

I sit on my bed and remember
Memories flood into my brain
The gatherings held each December
I cherish and hold dear

Though the years have past
And memories begin to fade
The pain will always last
I miss you every single day

I Was There

I was there for every event
When your first application was sent
For holidays, birthdays and graduations
All your overseas vacations
I was there when you cried
When you called out for me with tears in your eyes
I know you think of me often
I see your eyes, they soften
I feel the pain inside of you
And the emptiness there too
I wish I could take it all away
Tell you we'll be together someday
I am here, though you cannot see
Beside you I will always be

Alone

Alone I walk along
These narrow dirty halls
Trapped in my misery
Within these stone walls
I must find my daughter
Searching for her endlessly
She is not here, I cannot leave
I roam these halls restlessly
Standing in the window
I weep and drown in grief
Sometimes I think they see me
Though the glances are so brief
No one tries to help me
They do not think I am here
I yell and cry and try to be seen
Though no sound reaches the human ear
Forever I am doomed to walk
Among these crumbling old bones
No soul for company
Here alone, always alone

Ultimate Sacrifice

A chill across my face
Shivers creeping down my spine
Your presence I cannot deny
The love that once was mine

By day I walk among
Those who know not my pain
By night I see your pale form
Misty as a summer rain

Your once warm caress
Now icy tendrils on my skin
Your once bright blue eyes
Hide not the sorrow within

Forgive me my dear love
You paid my hefty price
Trading my life for yours
The ultimate sacrifice

Encounters

Have you ever had something happen?
Something you couldn't explain?
A breath on your neck,
The opening of a windowpane.
Or maybe a voice,
Whispering in your ear.
The books falling
But no one is here.
Or maybe you've seen
A figure walks down the hall.
Dark as night
Silent and tall.
Or maybe a mist
Transparent and white.
As it morphs and it floats
And gives you a fright.
There are many ways
One can experience the ghosts.
Some run away scared,
Another stands tall and boasts.
Have you ever had something happen?
Something you couldn't explain?
Something that scared you so badly?
Or made you feel ghostly pain?

Waverly Hills

Oh, Waverly Hills,
Despair you hold in these walls.
The sick, the insane, the poor
Daily rounds of pills
Screams still echo down these halls
The souls trapped forevermore

A darkness holds them here
An evil, huge black mass
Climbing walls, wreaking havoc
Oppressive forces instil fear
In all who dare pass
The threshold and turn the lock

I weep for these souls
The woman crying for help,
The little boy with his ball,
The nurse who lost control.
The screams, cries and yelps
The building shaking to its core

George

Tiptoe across the floor
Make sure nobody hears
Step over toy soldiers at war
Around the corne,r a shadow appears

Tap, tap, tap along the wall
Following the sound to our spot
Out from the tent rolls a ball
The clock chimes three o'clock

Into the play tent now
A blue face starts to appear
It is a kind of magic. Wow!
With him there is no fear

Whispers in the dark
The fake tea is served
On George's nec,k there is a mark
No doubt not deserved

George speaks strangely sometimes
His voice sounds far away
Often he speaks in rhyme
And is gone by break of day

But for now he is normal
Though see-through is he
He is always dressed so formal
My friend forever he will be

All night. Play, play, play
Taking turns with the toys
Wishing to play all day
And share with the other boys

But George says it’s not safe
For anyone to know he is here
It's a secret, it's unsafe
Whisper so they don't hear

George likes to joke
With the others in the house
A giggle here, there a poke
Sometimes scratching like a mouse

George is not happy, nor is he sad
Something has changed in him
Now he seems bad
He is angry, no longer grim

George is gone now
A dark man in his place
Is this George? How?
Three scratches on the face

House shaking, lights flickering
George is really mad
Try to run but he is quicker
He is very, very bad

George is not a friend
He is pure evil
A demon from Hell's end
Evil, evil, evil

All Is Silent

All is silent
The world is still
Then the Mel meter alarms
Excitement and fear invade the air
A voice screams from another room
A growl in the corner
Malicious or frightened is the question
Dark shapes dart through doors
Questions come in a flurry
Start off basic now
Who are you?
Are you stuck?
How many of you are there?
Silence
Review the recording
A whispering voice!
GET OUT!
It is angry
Snap, snap, snap
Will a figure be captured?
Oh, a shadow!
Can it be explained?
Debunked!
The team cast shadows
All night long, questions and captures

And then all of a sudden
Just before sunrise
All is silent

100 Years

One hundred years from now
When my body is in the ground
I will find my way back to this town
And wander all around
A spectre within the garden
As a couple passes my old house
I smile and wave and then
Walk silent as a mouse
Reflecting on the changes
The modern creeping in
The locks changed, old hinges
Gone, the shed no longer tin
One hundred years from now
I will return to this very spot
This to you is my vow
Though in flesh I will not

www.ingramcontent.com/pod-product-compliance
Lightning Source LLC
Chambersburg PA
CBHW051749130826
49812CB00033B/1062
* 9 7 8 9 3 5 7 4 4 8 0 6 2 *